"The Bible is strikingly ca [...]
reality that God's own pe [...]
lastingly. Where do we fi [...]
Christian teachers of our time, takes us deeply into the Psalms in a book
that will be of great encouragement to all believers. I am so thankful for
Ligon Duncan's devotion to God's word and the care of souls. Read this
book, and you will understand why."

> **R. Albert Mohler Jr.,** President, The Southern Baptist Theological
> Seminary

"Here is a book that is short enough for the person who is gripped by suffering to actually read and yet rich enough to meet that individual's need
for perspective and hope in the darkest of times."

> **Nancy Guthrie,** Bible teacher; author, *Hearing Jesus Speak into
> Your Sorrow*

"Ligon Duncan shows us beautifully how, even in our deepest despair, we
can have hope in God. We can run to him because he cares and understands. Through this book, Duncan continually lifts our gaze and reminds
us that no matter our circumstances, our great God is sympathetic, sovereign, and sufficient. Read this book for yourself, or make it a gift to those
struggling in their suffering. Here's the truth: You are not alone. The Lord
knows, and he hears."

> **Greg Gilbert,** Senior Pastor, Third Avenue Baptist Church,
> Louisville, Kentucky

"Don't let the brevity of this book fool you. It is packed with wisdom.
Ligon Duncan's insights from Psalms 88 and 89 are simple and fresh yet
at the same time moving and profound. *When Pain Is Real and God Seems
Silent* greatly encouraged me in my own suffering. I'd recommend it to
anyone who has felt confused, isolated, or forgotten in their pain and who
longs for a hope that endures."

> **Vaneetha Rendall Risner,** author, *The Scars That Have Shaped Me:
> How God Meets Us in Suffering*

"In the midst of our suffering we need a wake-up call to the truth that God's steadfast love never ceases. The Psalms are a gentle and real reminder that even in the hardest moments, God is there. Ligon Duncan offers a wonderful companion to two of the most honest psalms in the Bible. He helps us marvel at the beauty and wonder of our God as he is described in these psalms. We're reminded that our hope can be found only in God. Get out your Bible, read Psalms 88 and 89, and then read this short book. Your heart will be comforted by these truths."

Dave Furman, Senior Pastor, Redeemer Church of Dubai; author, *Being There* and *Kiss the Wave*

"With pastoral care and theological precision, Ligon Duncan guides us through Psalms 88 and 89 to help us better understand suffering. *When Pain Is Real and God Seems Silent* is an honest assessment of life in a fallen world with the hope we have in Christ. In this short and accessible book, Duncan steers clear of trite phrases and clichés and instead provides solid truth that will actually sustain us in trials."

Trillia Newbell, author, *Sacred Endurance*; *If God Is for Us*; and *Fear and Faith*

"Psalms of lament are missing in the church and in most believers' prayers. Ligon Duncan helps us recover this historic language in his careful and thoughtful examination of these two important psalms. Overflowing with pastoral instinct, rich exposition, and helpful application, this short book on Psalms 88 and 89 is long overdue."

Mark Vroegop, Lead Pastor, College Park Church, Indianapolis; author, *Dark Clouds, Deep Mercy: Discovering the Grace of Lament*

When Pain Is Real and God Seems Silent

When Pain Is Real and God Seems Silent

Finding Hope in the Psalms

Ligon Duncan

Foreword by Mark Dever

CROSSWAY®

WHEATON, ILLINOIS

When Pain Is Real and God Seems Silent: Finding Hope in the Psalms

Copyright © 2020 by Ligon Duncan

Published by Crossway
        1300 Crescent Street
        Wheaton, Illinois 60187

Cover design: Dan Farrell

Cover image: Lithograph by Étienne Léopold Trouvelot

First printing 2020

Printed in the United States of America

Unless otherwise indicated, Scripture quotations are from the ESV® Bible (The Holy Bible, English Standard Version®), copyright © 2001 by Crossway, a publishing ministry of Good News Publishers. Used by permission. All rights reserved.

Scripture quotations marked NASB are from *The New American Standard Bible®*. Copyright © The Lockman Foundation 1960, 1962, 1963, 1968, 1971, 1972, 1973, 1975, 1977, 1995. Used by permission.

All emphases in Scripture quotations have been added by the author.

Trade paperback ISBN: 978-1-4335-6905-0
ePub ISBN: 978-1-4335-6908-1
PDF ISBN: 978-1-4335-6906-7
Mobipocket ISBN: 978-1-4335-6907-4

Library of Congress Cataloging-in-Publication Data

Names: Duncan, J. Ligon, 1960– author. | Dever, Mark.
Title: When pain is real and God seems silent : finding hope in the Psalms / J. Ligon Duncan ; foreword by Mark Dever.
Description: Wheaton, Illinois : Crossway, 2020. | Includes bibliographical references and index.
Identifiers: LCCN 2019029589 (print) | LCCN 2019029590 (ebook) | ISBN 9781433569050 (trade paperback) | ISBN 9781433569067 (pdf) | ISBN 9781433569074 (mobi) | ISBN 9781433569081 (epub)
Subjects: LCSH: Bible. Psalms, LXXXVIII–LXXXIX—Criticism, interpretation, etc. | Suffering—Biblical teaching. | Pain—Biblical teaching.
Classification: LCC BS1430.6.S8 D86 2020 (print) | LCC BS1430.6.S8 (ebook) | DDC 223/.206—dc23
LC record available at https://lccn.loc.gov/2019029589
LC ebook record available at https://lccn.loc.gov/2019029590

Crossway is a publishing ministry of Good News Publishers.

LB		29	28	27	26	25	24	23	22	21	20
15	14	13	12	11	10	9	8	7	6	5	4	3	2	1

Contents

Foreword

In 1895 Andrew Murray was staying as a guest in a home while traveling for preaching. One morning, he lay in bed because his back, injured a few years prior, was causing him severe pain. When his hostess brought him breakfast, she told him that a troubled woman had come to the house asking for his counsel. Murray handed her a piece of paper and said, "Just give her this advice I'm writing down for myself; it may be that she'll find it helpful." This is what was written:

In time of trouble say, "First, He brought me here. It is by His will I am in this strait place; in that I will rest." Next, "He will keep me here in His love, and give me grace in this trial to behave as His child." Then say, "He will make the trial a blessing, teaching me lessons He intends me to learn, and working in me the grace He means to bestow." And last, say, "In His good time He can bring me out again. How, and when, He knows." Therefore say, "I am here (1) by God's appointment, (2) in His keeping, (3) under His training, (4) for His time."[1]

Psalms 88 and 89 are about suffering. Psalm 88 is about individual suffering, and Psalm 89 is about corporate suffering, or suffering together. Ligon Duncan preached sermons on both of these psalms a few years apart at our church—Capitol Hill Baptist Church—in Washington, DC. You may still hear the original sermons at our church's website (www .capbap.org).

Each sermon was fresh and full of truth and empathy. Each one was delivered powerfully and, at points, with loving tears. The compassion of our heavenly Father was appearing before us in his inspired word being preached to us with such care and feeling. Both times I thought not only of our benefiting from God's word so preached but of how so many others could as well, if we would simply reduce these sermons to print and then edit and publish them. And here they are.

Having just read over them both, I am again moved by the power of these two psalms and by the simple, clear, and yet profound and sympathetic wisdom our God has shown us by inspiring them and including them in the book of Psalms. Everyone suffers. Everyone is confused by suffering. Part of that confusion is a sense of uniqueness and isolation. "No one else feels like this. Who would understand what I'm going through here?"

In these two brief meditations, the thoughts of Heman and Ethan, two Ezrahites, are brought before us and examined. They are placed before us through Ligon Duncan's clear explanation and simple illustrations. As in these psalms, examples of suffering are given not as contradictions to a belief in God's sovereignty but as the variety of circumstances through which God may be trusted. The very darkness of the experience provides a dramatic background for the reemergence of hope.

Reflecting on the missionary life of Hudson Taylor, Dr. and Mrs. Howard Taylor observed that we experience "love first, then suffering, then a deeper love—thus only can God's work be done."[2] Psalms 88 and 89 remind us of this truth, help us see our sufferings, and then help us see our way through, with hope intact and faith—miraculously—deepened. May such be your experience as you read these two brief messages.

Thankful to the preacher and to the psalmists, we are most thankful for the God to whom they complained and in whom they rightly trusted.

Mark Dever
Capitol Hill Baptist Church
Washington, DC
July 2019

1

Psalm 88

A Song. A Psalm of the Sons of Korah. To the choirmaster:
according to Mahalath Leannoth. A Maskil of Heman the
Ezrahite.

O Lord, God of my salvation,
    I cry out day and night before you.
Let my prayer come before you;
    incline your ear to my cry!

For my soul is full of troubles,
    and my life draws near to Sheol.
I am counted among those who go down to the pit;
    I am a man who has no strength,
like one set loose among the dead,
    like the slain that lie in the grave,
like those whom you remember no more,
    for they are cut off from your hand.
You have put me in the depths of the pit,
    in the regions dark and deep.

Your wrath lies heavy upon me,
  and you overwhelm me with all your waves.   *Selah*

You have caused my companions to shun me;
  you have made me a horror to them.
I am shut in so that I cannot escape;
  my eye grows dim through sorrow.
Every day I call upon you, O LORD;
  I spread out my hands to you.
Do you work wonders for the dead?
  Do the departed rise up to praise you?   *Selah*
Is your steadfast love declared in the grave,
  or your faithfulness in Abaddon?
Are your wonders known in the darkness,
  or your righteousness in the land of forgetfulness?

But I, O LORD, cry to you;
  in the morning my prayer comes before you.
O LORD, why do you cast my soul away?
  Why do you hide your face from me?
Afflicted and close to death from my youth up,
  I suffer your terrors; I am helpless.
Your wrath has swept over me;
  your dreadful assaults destroy me.
They surround me like a flood all day long;
  they close in on me together.
You have caused my beloved and my friend to shun me;
  my companions have become darkness.

Psalm 88 is perhaps the most tragic psalm in all Scripture—no psalm is sadder. As one commentator writes, "This psalm is full of the dread of death as the psalmist laments his condition as one who is doomed to die."[1] Or as Matthew Henry has noted,

> This psalm is a lamentation, one of the most melancholy of all the psalms; and it does not conclude, as usually the melancholy psalms do, with the least intimation of comfort or joy, but, from first to last, it is mourning and woe.[2]

Historically, Christians have loved the Psalms because they express our deepest emotions and put into words our most severe experiences. At the same time, most psalms, even those that focus on suffering or sorrow, contain some explicit notes of redemption. No matter how low the psalmists get, most psalms of lament end with at least some spark of hope or word of grace. But not this one. The tone of Psalm 88 is unwaveringly dark.

That fact in itself is important. Psalm 88 describes what many Christians know to be true. Christians face troubles, often abiding, intractable ones. Our Lord himself warned us that we would encounter difficulty as we followed him. Yet despite Scripture's warnings, many Christians still feel confused and bewildered when they encounter various trials (James 1:2).

False teachers often capitalize on the suffering of Christians to promote false doctrine. For instance, prosperity-gospel peddlers assert that if you simply had enough faith, your troubles would go away. Obviously, we need only look to the examples of the apostle Paul and of the Lord himself to demonstrate just how false these sentiments are.

At the same time, many well-meaning Christians regrettably offer similar advice to suffering saints, encouraging those in great pain simply to "let go and trust God more—move on with life." Of course, it's never a bad idea to trust God or to encourage others to do the same. But as we minister to the suffering, we must also lend a sympathetic ear and exercise great patience. People must process pain and sorrow, not simply "let go" of it.

Even more troubling, some Christians buy into the lie that believers never live with unanswered prayer or unrelieved suffering. And yet this psalm shows quite the opposite. Sometimes God ordains that believers endure chronic pain and chooses never to relieve them of their thorn in the flesh (2 Cor. 12:7–10).

This psalm is unremittingly dark. And the psalmist never *explicitly* articulates a hope of redemption. But even in the midst of this dark and melancholy psalm, even in the midst of the lamentation and tears, if we look carefully enough and read this psalm in the context of all Scripture, we can still find a glimmer of hope and a few lessons God in hard times.

What Can Miserable Christians Sing?

Several years ago, Carl Trueman wrote an article asking a provocative question: "What Can Miserable Christians Sing?" As Trueman notes, most of the songs Christians sing in church express only happiness—or even worse, a trite and chipper attitude toward the Christian life. Our songs are exclusively happy, as if that were the only emotion Christians ought to experience. But what do miserable Christians sing? Trueman argues that Christians should look once again to the Psalms as a way of expressing sorrow and lament:

> The psalms, the Bible's own hymnbook, have almost entirely dropped from view in the contemporary Western evangelical scene. I am not certain about why this should be, but I have an instinctive feel that it has more than a little to do with the fact that a high proportion of the psalter is taken up with lamentation, with feeling sad, unhappy, tormented, and broken. In modern Western culture, these are simply not emotions which have much credibility: sure, people still feel these things, but to admit that they are a normal part of one's everyday life is tantamount to admitting that one has failed in today's health, wealth, and happiness society. And, of

course, if one does admit to them, one must neither accept them nor take any personal responsibility for them: one must blame one's parents, sue one's employer, pop a pill, or check into a clinic in order to have such dysfunctional emotions soothed and one's self-image restored. . . .

In the psalms, God has given the church a language which allows it to express even the deepest agonies of the human soul in the context of worship.[3]

So what do Christians sing when despondent, depressed, or discouraged? Psalm 88 is, in part, an answer to that question.

Surveying the Psalm: Four Observations

Perhaps you think that Christians *shouldn't* experience despair—or at least you assume that godly, mature Christians won't ever feel that way. And yet, consider the author of this psalm. According to the heading, this psalm was written by Heman the Ezrahite. Heman is mentioned throughout the Old Testament as a man who led the people of God in worship, a poet-theologian par excellence. According to 1 Kings 4:31, Heman the Ezrahite was one of the five wisest men in his generation. He was renowned for his depth, insight, and maturity.

Yet for Heman the Ezrahite, all the lights had gone out. Despite his constant prayer, his life situation seemed to attest to only one thing: "Your God does not hear you." Psalm 88 is the portrait of a godly man crying to the Lord in great suffering—and seeing no light at the end of the tunnel.

Some of the most extraordinary Christians I have ever met have found themselves in exactly the same place as Heman the Ezrahite. Whether through debilitating illness, personal tragedy, or persecution, these Christians have endured years of suffering, all while waiting on God to respond to unanswered prayer.

Are you in a similar situation? Can you identify with the tears of this psalm? If so, this psalm has something important to teach us about God and hard times. Consider these four observations from the psalm.

The Psalmist Knows the Pain of Unanswered Prayer

O Lord, God of my salvation,
  I cry out day and night before you.
Let my prayer come before you;
  incline your ear to my cry! (Ps. 88:1–2)

Heman is a godly man, but here we find him hopeless and desperate. He describes his prayer as a "cry"—an urgent and serious petition to the Lord. Yet despite his urgency, his prayer is met with deafening silence. The Lord seems not to hear him.

Have you ever assumed that mature believers always have their prayers answered? Have you ever thought that godly men and women don't endure suffering? Well, the Bible teaches just the opposite. Sometimes even mature, godly believers—believers like Heman the Ezrahite—feel as if their cries for help go unheard by our Lord.

The Psalmist Knows That God Is
Sovereign over His Suffering

> For my soul is full of troubles,
>> and my life draws near to Sheol.
> I am counted among those who go down to the pit;
>> I am a man who has no strength,
> like one set loose among the dead,
>> like the slain that lie in the grave,
> like those whom you remember no more,
>> for they are cut off from your hand.
> You have put me in the depths of the pit,
>> in the regions dark and deep.
> Your wrath lies heavy upon me,
>> and you overwhelm me with all your waves. *Selah*
>
> You have caused my companions to shun me;
>> you have made me a horror to them.
> I am shut in so that I cannot escape;
>> my eye grows dim through sorrow.
> Every day I call upon you, O LORD;
>> I spread out my hands to you. (Ps. 88:3–9)

Though Heman feels unheard and wonders whether God cares for him, he is also absolutely certain that God is sovereign over his suffering. In verses 3–9, he explicitly attributes his suffering to the hand of God. Consider how often he speaks of God's agency in his trials:

- "You have put me in the depths of the pit." (v. 6)
- "Your wrath lies heavy upon me." (v. 7)
- "You overwhelm me with all your waves." (v. 7)
- "You have caused my companions to shun me." (v. 8)
- "You have made me a horror to them." (v. 8)

Unlike many modern theologians, the psalmist is not trying to get God "off the hook" when it comes to suffering. He does not reject that God is loving, nor does he reject that God is sovereign. He never considers for an instant that God is not in control.

Very often, when we encounter severe trials and suffering, we are tempted to think that our situation is somehow out of God's hands. Some people even encourage us to doubt God's sovereignty: "Oh, God had nothing to do with that tragedy. He didn't know that it was coming." Yet Heman, one of the five wisest men in all Israel, never entertained that idea. He believed God was in charge of everything, including his troubles. He coped with his suffering by fearfully acknowledging God as the sovereign one who rules heaven and earth, including his own suffering.

The Psalmist Asks Searching Questions

> Do you work wonders for the dead?
>> Do the departed rise up to praise you?   *Selah*
> Is your steadfast love declared in the grave,
>> or your faithfulness in Abaddon?
> Are your wonders known in the darkness,
>> or your righteousness in the land of forgetfulness?
>> (Ps. 88:10–12)

In these words, the psalmist is asking, "How can I live for your glory, O God, if I'm dead?" This question shows us quite a bit about Heman. He knows he was put on this earth to glorify God; he knows he has been created to praise the Lord in all of life. But how can he do that if he's dead? Heman's logic is certainly understandable. How can God glorify himself among the dead? Dead men don't have prayers answered. Dead men aren't delivered from trial. Dead men can't sing the Lord's praises.

Strikingly, even in the midst of his pain, Heman has not forgotten the reason why he was created. These questions come not from doubt but from faith. Heman is not wrestling with whether God's word is true; he is trying to square what he knows to be true about God with his own experience.

The Psalmist Keeps His Eyes Fixed on God

> But I, O LORD, cry to you;
>> in the morning my prayer comes before you.

O LORD, why do you cast my soul away?
    Why do you hide your face from me?
Afflicted and close to death from my youth up,
    I suffer your terrors; I am helpless.
Your wrath has swept over me;
    your dreadful assaults destroy me.
They surround me like a flood all day long;
    they close in on me together.
You have caused my beloved and my friend to shun me;
    my companions have become darkness.
        (Ps. 88:13–18)

Finally, Heman returns to his unanswered prayer, this time with two more probing questions: (1) Why am I still waiting for help? and (2) Why you, O Lord? I often ask the question, Why me? Heman asks, Why you, O Lord? As he writes in verse 14,

Why do you cast my soul away?
    Why do you hide your face from me?

The psalmist may not know why he is suffering, but he knows God is behind it—and that he has a purpose in it.

Four Lessons for Suffering Well

Psalm 88 teaches us a number of important lessons about God and hard times. Not everyone gets a happy ending in a fallen world—and that includes even godly believers. Unrelieved suffering sometimes continues even until the very end of our lives. Mature believers can experience profound dissatisfaction with life. We also learn that some believers endure enormous suffering and still maintain their commitment to the Lord. God's grace sustains us, even in the darkest hours, so that we never give up.

But this psalm holds out even more lessons of hope than we might first realize. Embedded even in this darkest of psalms are a few notes of light and redemption. Where? Let me propose four ways this psalm emboldens our hope and encourages us in suffering.

Divine Revelation

Consider the astounding fact that this psalm is in the Bible. Imagine being able to speak to Heman the Ezrahite and telling him that his lament is part of Scripture, preserved for thousands of years in God's word so that other followers of the Lord might know how to bare their soul to God. What might Heman realize? He would realize that the Lord did hear him! The Lord not only heard these words, he inspired them so that other Christians might sing them in the coming ages to express their own sorrow to God. Heman would also recognize that other followers of the Lord share the same troubles and carry the same burdens. Consider just how many believers since Heman's time have sung these words, sharing their grief with his.

Friend, your life may be filled with far more suffering than my own, but Scripture teaches that your troubles don't belong to you alone. God placed psalms of lament, like this one, in Scripture so that we could all learn how to cry to the Lord in our sadness and grief together. Psalms like this one teach us to share in one another's suffering and to bear one another's burdens.

God's Character

Notice how the psalmist describes the character of God. Heman, even in his agony, still comforts himself with the character of God: "O Lord, God of my salvation" (Ps. 88:1). With this description of God, the psalmist acknowledges God as his only help and hope—the only source of salvation. No matter what else might be taken from us, this hope in the character of God cannot be taken away. Our circumstances never alter God's character.

Many times in the Christian life, God answers our cries "Why, O Lord?" not by explaining his providence but by giving us a deeper understanding of his person. In other words, when we cry, "Lord, why are you doing this?" he often answers by saying, "Let me show you who I am." And if you see him, he will be enough.

God's Glory

Observe how the psalmist endeavors to live for God's glory even in his suffering. In Psalm 88:10–12 we find the psalmist asking, "How am I going to live for your glory when I'm dead?" These probing questions reveal a heart that wants God glorified. As Derek Kidner writes,

> This author, like Job, does not give up. He completes his prayer, still in the dark and totally unrewarded. The taunt, "Does Job fear God for naught?" is answered yet again. Like Job, the author has received no satisfactory answer for why his life has turned out as miserably as it has. But also, like Job, he does not "curse God and die" (Job 2:9). Rather, he is seen clinging to God.[4]

We can learn two important points from this observation. First, we must remember never to allow suffering to make us bitter toward life or cold toward the glory of God. When I encounter suffering, my first inclination is to think, "Why is this happening? God's not in control!" But we must always remember that the Lord has both warned us to prepare for suffering and appointed trouble for his people for their everlasting good and for his glory. This psalmist's heart reflects a right posture toward God: he cries for relief from his troubles even as he acknowledges that they come from God's hand.

Second, we learn that the trouble we endure in this life should not call into question the genuineness of God's love. Instead, these troubles prove God's love. Consider these astounding passages from Scripture:

> For I consider that the sufferings of this present time are not worth comparing with the glory that is to be revealed to us. (Rom. 8:18)

> For it has been granted to you that for the sake of Christ you should not only believe in him but also suffer for his sake. (Phil. 1:29)

Our sonship, our adoption, our being the children of God is actually proved in our troubles. Charles Simeon once beautifully captured this truth:

> There are some who by God Himself are brought into manifold temptations, and are suffered to experience much darkness in their souls. And though at first sight it should seem as if these persons were less beloved of the Lord than others, the truth is that they are often to be found amongst those who are his chief favorites: "Whom the Lord loves, He chasteneth;" and usually, those most, who are most beloved.[5]

Could your Lord be speaking his love into your heart in your deepest trouble? Echoing the words of the hymn

"How Firm a Foundation?" ask God to "sanctify to you your deepest distress."[6]

Eternal Perspective

Take comfort from the fact that the sufferings of this life are the worst you will ever endure. If you know Christ and have come to him in faith and repentance, then your suffering has an end. The trials of this life are the worst things you will ever endure.

But friend, if you don't know Christ, then you are alone in your suffering. You are in a far, far worse place than this psalmist. The hopelessness experienced by this psalmist was only apparent and temporary. But those who die without repenting of their sin will know true hopelessness, that which is real and eternal. Hell has no light at the end of the tunnel. If you do not know Christ, then let your sufferings show you your need for a Savior. If you are already a Christian, then let your own suffering remind you that you are an undeserving, hell-bound sinner saved by God's mercy. Let that thought drive you to share the gospel with those around you so that they, too, might be saved from never-ending hopelessness.

Our Suffering and the Suffering of Jesus

This dark psalm has one more glimmer of hope. The suffering of this psalm ultimately points to the sufferings of Jesus. Notice the parallels between this psalm and the sorrows of our

Lord. The psalmist records that his "soul is full of troubles" (Ps. 88:3), even as he desires to glorify the Lord (vv. 10–12). So also, our Lord, on his final trip to Jerusalem, says, "Now is my soul troubled" (John 12:27), even as he affirms his continued desire to glorify God (v. 28).

Again, in Matthew 26:38–39, we find Jesus in the garden of Gethsemane saying that his soul is "sorrowful, even to death." He even prays, "My Father, if it be possible, let this cup pass from me; nevertheless, not as I will, but as you will." Finally, Jesus's agony culminates on the cross as he cries out, "My God, My God, why have you forsaken me?" (Matt. 27:46). Now listen to the language of Psalm 88 one more time:

> *You* have put me in the lowest pit. . . .
> *Your* wrath has rested upon me;
>> *You* have afflicted me. . . .
> *You* have removed my [companions] . . . ;
>> *You* have made me an object of loathing. . . .
>
> Why do *you* reject my soul?
>> Why do *you* hide your face from me? . . .
>> I suffer *your* terrors. . . .
> *Your* burning anger has passed over me;
>> *Your* terrors have destroyed me. . . .
> *You* have removed lover and friend far from me.
>> (vv. 6–8, 14–16, 18 NASB)

Jesus's words and life attest to these very sufferings on the cross.

Christian, when you find yourself in trouble like that described in Psalm 88, you are being granted by the Father just a tiny taste of what Christ endured for you to the full. He was "a man of sorrows and acquainted with grief" (Isa. 53:3). Was there ever any sorrow like his? Your troubles pale in comparison to the burden he bore. This psalm ultimately points to Jesus's suffering for you.

This encouragement would be enough, but we find yet more. Remember that in Psalm 88 Heman asks a question:

> Do you work wonders for the dead?
> Do the departed rise up to praise you?   *Selah*
> Is your steadfast love declared in the grave? (vv. 10–12)

God's answer is "Yes! Yes, I will do all these things!" God ultimately answers the despair that concludes this psalm by resurrecting Jesus from the dead. In Jesus's death and resurrection, God has performed wonders and caused departed spirits to rise and praise him. His loving-kindness will indeed be declared by those once in graves. In Christ's resurrection we have the hope of deliverance from death. He is the firstfruits of a resurrection that will one day include all those who have trusted in him. Psalm 88 may be the darkest psalm in the Psalter, perhaps the darkest chapter in all Scripture. But because of the work of our Lord Jesus Christ, there is a light of hope even here that will never go out.

Psalm 89

A Maskil of Ethan the Ezrahite.

I will sing of the steadfast love of the LORD, forever;
    with my mouth I will make known your faithfulness
       to all generations.
For I said, "Steadfast love will be built up forever;
    in the heavens you will establish your faithfulness."
You have said, "I have made a covenant with my
       chosen one;
    I have sworn to David my servant:
'I will establish your offspring forever,
    and build your throne for all generations.'"   *Selah*

Let the heavens praise your wonders, O LORD,
    your faithfulness in the assembly of the holy ones!
For who in the skies can be compared to the LORD?
    Who among the heavenly beings is like the LORD,

a God greatly to be feared in the council of the holy
ones,
and awesome above all who are around him?
O Lord God of hosts,
who is mighty as you are, O Lord,
with your faithfulness all around you?
You rule the raging of the sea;
when its waves rise, you still them.
You crushed Rahab like a carcass;
you scattered your enemies with your mighty arm.
The heavens are yours; the earth also is yours;
the world and all that is in it, you have founded
them.
The north and the south, you have created them;
Tabor and Hermon joyously praise your name.
You have a mighty arm;
strong is your hand, high your right hand.
Righteousness and justice are the foundation of your
throne;
steadfast love and faithfulness go before you.
Blessed are the people who know the festal shout,
who walk, O Lord, in the light of your face,
who exult in your name all the day
and in your righteousness are exalted.
For you are the glory of their strength;
by your favor our horn is exalted.

For our shield belongs to the LORD,
>   our king to the Holy One of Israel.

Of old you spoke in a vision to your godly one, and said:
>   "I have granted help to one who is mighty;
>   I have exalted one chosen from the people.
I have found David, my servant;
>   with my holy oil I have anointed him,
so that my hand shall be established with him;
>   my arm also shall strengthen him.
The enemy shall not outwit him;
>   the wicked shall not humble him.
I will crush his foes before him
>   and strike down those who hate him.
My faithfulness and my steadfast love shall be
>   with him,
>   and in my name shall his horn be exalted.
I will set his hand on the sea
>   and his right hand on the rivers.
He shall cry to me, 'You are my Father,
>   my God, and the Rock of my salvation.'
And I will make him the firstborn,
>   the highest of the kings of the earth.
My steadfast love I will keep for him forever,
>   and my covenant will stand firm for him.
I will establish his offspring forever
>   and his throne as the days of the heavens.

If his children forsake my law
    and do not walk according to my rules,
if they violate my statutes
    and do not keep my commandments,
then I will punish their transgression with the rod
    and their iniquity with stripes,
but I will not remove from him my steadfast love
    or be false to my faithfulness.
I will not violate my covenant
    or alter the word that went forth from my lips.
Once for all I have sworn by my holiness;
    I will not lie to David.
His offspring shall endure forever,
    his throne as long as the sun before me.
Like the moon it shall be established forever,
    a faithful witness in the skies."   *Selah*

But now you have cast off and rejected;
    you are full of wrath against your anointed.
You have renounced the covenant with your servant;
    you have defiled his crown in the dust.
You have breached all his walls;
    you have laid his strongholds in ruins.
All who pass by plunder him;
    he has become the scorn of his neighbors.
You have exalted the right hand of his foes;
    you have made all his enemies rejoice.

You have also turned back the edge of his sword,
    and you have not made him stand in battle.
You have made his splendor to cease
    and cast his throne to the ground.
You have cut short the days of his youth;
    you have covered him with shame.   *Selah*

How long, O Lord? Will you hide yourself forever?
    How long will your wrath burn like fire?
Remember how short my time is!
    For what vanity you have created all the children
        of man!
What man can live and never see death?
    Who can deliver his soul from the power of Sheol?
                             Selah

Lord, where is your steadfast love of old,
    which by your faithfulness you swore to David?
Remember, O Lord, how your servants are mocked,
    and how I bear in my heart the insults of all the
        many nations,
with which your enemies mock, O Lord,
    with which they mock the footsteps of your
        anointed.

Blessed be the Lord forever!
    Amen and Amen.

John Calvin once described the Psalms as the "anatomy of all the Parts of the Soul."[1] What he meant was that every experience we may encounter in the Christian life can be found in the Psalms. They give us words to express joy, loss, anxiety, fear, sadness, thankfulness, and grief. They put words to the deepest feelings of our heart—and even teach us how to sing those feelings back to God himself.

Psalm 89 is a well-known psalm. Yet I confess that I misunderstood it for fifty years. Why? I remember singing a part of this psalm as a child. Perhaps you're familiar with it:

I will sing of the mercies of the Lord forever,
I will sing, I will sing.
I will sing of the mercies of the Lord forever,
I will sing of the mercies of the Lord.

With my mouth will I make known
Thy faithfulness, thy faithfulness.
With my mouth will I make known
Thy faithfulness to all generations.[2]

That song is obviously based on Psalm 89:1. But the timbre of that melody can be a bit misleading. If you're familiar with the tune, you know that it's a happy one—even chipper. But as verses 38–51 of this psalm show, these words were originally meant to be sung not in a cheerful tone but through blinding tears. This psalm was written not in the good times but in the bad. It was penned by Ethan the Ezrahite, a contemporary of Solomon, most likely when the kingdom of Israel divided during the reign of Rehoboam, Solomon's son. The ten northern tribes rejected the rule of David's sons over them and formed their own kingdom under Jeroboam, bringing into question God's promises to David and his line. The great kingdom David had established had fallen into tatters.

Later generations of Jews found that this psalm gave voice to their harrowing experience too. The children of Israel thus sang this song when their nation had been destroyed and the people themselves were being held captive—exiled in Babylon. At the time of the exile, the world, for Israel, had basically come to an end. The Davidic kingdom was broken. The people had been deported to a foreign land. The promises given to Abraham seemed a distant memory, a hope long forgotten. In this situation Israel again asked, "Has God reneged on his promise to David? Has he forgotten us? Have the promises to Abraham and David failed? What is going on?"

In the Davidic covenant, in 2 Samuel 7, God promised David that his family would reign forever (vv. 13, 16). When the kingdom divided, the reign of David's line appeared to be on the brink of dissolution. God upheld David's royal line so that by the time of the exile, the Davidic dynasty had reigned for four hundred years—one of the longest continuous reigns of any single dynasty in world history. But God did not promise David that his people would reign for a long time; he promised David that his line would reign forever. At the time of the exile, the crown of David lay "in the dust" (Ps. 89:39), and his throne had been cast to the ground (v. 44). How could Israel process what had happened? How could they make sense of the world when God didn't seem to deliver on his promises?

It's not hard to identify with Israel's befuddlement. Hard times often make us question God's goodness. We're even tempted to consider whether God will indeed be faithful to his promises. So what do we do when all our hopes have been dashed? What do we do when the promises of God seem not to come to pass?

Thankfully, this psalm provides us with hope and with marching orders for how we can continue to trust the Lord, even as the world seems to unravel around us. Consider three hope-filled observations from the text, three doctrines the psalmist holds dear in suffering, and the one glorious gospel at the foundation of it all.

Three Hope-Filled Observations from Psalm 89

Suffering with Hope

The promises of God do not exempt us from suffering and calamity; instead, they enable us to suffer with hope. How can the psalmist sing of the steadfast love of the Lord (Ps.

89:1) even while he asks God, "Where is your steadfast love of old" (v. 49)? How can the psalmist recount the history of God's promises to David in the first thirty-seven verses, even while it seems that those promises lie trampled in the dust with David's crown and throne? The psalmist recognizes that the promises of God enable him to endure suffering with hope that the Lord will eventually make good on his word.

We find this same truth throughout Scripture. God loved Job. In fact, if I can put it this way, God was even proud of Job. Just consider how God speaks about him to Satan in Job 1:8: "Have you considered my servant Job, that there is none like him on the earth, a blameless and upright man, who fears God and turns away from evil?" And yet, even God's love for Job did not exempt him from suffering.

We find the same is true today. God loved Job, but he still suffered. God made glorious promises to Abraham, David, and the nation of Israel, but they still endured terrible trials. Christians today, bought by the blood of Christ, know deep and abiding sorrows and suffering in this world. God's promises don't spare us from suffering and calamity, but they do give us reason to hope.

Praising God

Despite his suffering and perplexity, the psalmist continues to praise God. Had I written Psalm 89, I imagine it would look quite different. Unlike Ethan the Ezrahite, I'm not sure I could have waited thirty-seven verses to get to my complaints and requests. But this psalmist understands something important—it's always time to praise the Lord. Even though his eyes are swollen with tears, Ethan the Ezrahite spends the majority of this psalm singing the Lord's praises.

In fact, as you look throughout Scripture, you find that God's people often praise the Lord even in the worst of circumstances. The apostles "rejoiced" when they were beaten by the Sanhedrin for evangelizing (Acts 5:41). Paul and Silas sang hymns in prison (Acts 16:25). When Peter addressed the persecuted and marginalized exiled Christians in Asia Minor, he invited them to bless the Lord and sing the doxology (1 Pet. 1:3–5).

Praising God in the midst of pain is one of the most profound testimonies that a believer or a congregation can ever give to the Lord. No pain or heartbreak should ever take praise from our lips. I'll never forget the glorious and courageous faith of a godly woman in my former church named Margaret. After hearing about an emergency in her family, I rushed to Blair Batson Hospital's intensive-care unit. I was there with the family when her two-year-old boy died in her arms. With a mother's love and a Christian's faith, she looked at me through tears and asked, "Ligon, can we sing the doxology?" Like Job, she confessed, "The LORD gave, and the

Lord has taken away; blessed be the name of the Lord" (Job 1:21).

God's people know profound pain, but no circumstance can make God one bit less worthy of our praise. God is worthy of our worship simply because of who he is. Our worship is ultimately rooted in his character, not our circumstances.

Submitting to God's Providence

We must submit our lives to God's good and mysterious providence. The psalmist never claims to have an answer for his suffering. He never pretends to understand God's mysterious purposes. He is perplexed by the Lord's works. Just look at his exasperated cries at the end of Psalm 89:

> How long, O Lord? Will you hide yourself forever?
> > How long will your wrath burn like fire? (v. 46)

> Lord, where is your steadfast love of old,
> > which by your faithfulness you swore to David?
> > > (v. 49)

But no answer is forthcoming. The psalmist receives no response to these desperate cries. And yet, he trusts God. How do we know? Because these questions are addressed to God! The psalmist recognizes that God is the Lord of history. He takes his complaints to the Lord, not to any other. He addresses himself to the one whose providence oversees all creation, even when that providence leaves him utterly perplexed. Similarly, in trying circumstances, we must submit ourselves to the Lord of history, looking only to him for answers, comfort, and hope.

William Cowper, an eighteenth-century English poet and hymn writer, captured this submissive posture in his famous hymn "God Moves in a Mysterious Way." Cowper knew firsthand what it meant to suffer under a mysterious providence. He was plagued with some kind of bipolar disorder and extreme depression. On a number of occasions he even attempted suicide. Cowper's hymn captures both the darkness of his circumstances and the faithfulness of God in mysterious providence:

> God moves in a mysterious way
> His wonders to perform;
> He plants His footsteps in the sea
> And rides upon the storm.
>
> Deep in unfathomable mines
> Of never failing skill
> He treasures up His bright designs
> And works His sov'reign will.
>
> Ye fearful saints, fresh courage take;
> The clouds ye so much dread
> Are big with mercy and shall break
> In blessings on your head.

Judge not the Lord by feeble sense,
But trust Him for His grace;
Behind a frowning providence
He hides a smiling face.

His purposes will ripen fast,
Unfolding every hour;
The bud may have a bitter taste,
But sweet will be the flow'r.

Blind unbelief is sure to err
And scan His work in vain;
God is His own interpreter,
And He will make it plain.[3]

Cowper's imagery is startling. God's footsteps are "planted in the sea"—a place that leaves no footprints. We can't see where his feet have come from or where they're going. His plans are hidden in "unfathomable mines"—unsearchable and undiscovered. Yet Cowper's exhortations to his own soul are equally startling. Halfway through the song he preaches to himself to take "fresh courage" and "judge not the Lord by feeble sense, but trust Him for His grace," because "behind a frowning providence he hides a smiling face." Cowper, like this psalm, is reminding us that we are poor interpreters of God's providence. While we may not understand *what* God is doing, we can always trust *who* he is. We must never interpret God's character by our circumstances. We must instead interpret our circumstances by God's character.

Three Doctrines That Sustain Us in Suffering

As we look closely, we also find three doctrines that undergird the psalmist's hope in God and that sustain him in the midst of his suffering.

The Doctrine of Election

First, we find the psalmist taking comfort from the doctrine of election. The doctrine of election is not an esoteric theological point for seminarians to fight about. Election in Scripture is meant to generate both hope *for* the people of God and worshiping hearts *in* the people of God. Notice how the psalmist celebrates God on account of his electing grace:

> I will sing of the steadfast love of the LORD, forever;
>> with my mouth I will make known your faithfulness
>>> to all generations. . . .
> You have said, "I have made a covenant with my
>> chosen one;
>> I have sworn to David my servant . . ." (Ps. 89:1, 3)

The psalmist celebrates God's steadfast love, his electing love, that he showed to David and his offspring. God chose David over his brothers, appointed him to be king, anointed him as the ruler of Israel, and promised him a dynasty—and he did all this on his own initiative. God chose David not because of something in him but because of God's inscrutable and wise purpose.

The doctrine of election should cultivate hope and joy in the Christian life. Jesus himself employed this doctrine to comfort his disciples. In the upper room, he reminded them, "You did not choose me, but I chose you" (John 15:16). Why did he remind them of this truth? They were all about to fail him and abandon him, even in his moment of greatest need. As they had to process their own shame and guilt for abandoning Christ, Jesus wanted the doctrine of election to ring in their ears and bring them comfort: "You did not choose me, but I chose you." Their love may prove fickle, inconstant, and weak. But his never changes.

The Doctrine of the Covenant of Grace

God's covenant of grace is the outworking of his salvific promises throughout redemptive history. In the covenant of grace, God enters into relationship with his people. The promises given to David in 2 Samuel 7 are part of that covenant, which the psalmist repeatedly recalls throughout Psalm 89:

> You have said, "I have made a covenant with my
> chosen one;
> I have sworn to David my servant . . ." (v. 3)

My steadfast love I will keep for him forever,
    and my covenant will stand firm for him. (v. 28)

I will not violate my covenant
    or alter the word that went forth from my lips.
        (v. 34)

Once for all I have sworn by my holiness;
    I will not lie to David. (v. 35)

Lord, where is your steadfast love of old,
    which by your faithfulness you swore to David? (v. 49)

When God enters into covenant with his people, he binds himself to them by an oath. The covenant of grace, which he swore to David, his offspring, and the people of Israel, is not just a pledge that David's descendants will reign forever. In the covenant of grace, God pledges himself to his people: "I will be your God, and you shall be my people" (Jer. 7:23; cf. Ex. 6:7; 2 Sam. 7:16).

Have you ever wondered what God wants out of your salvation? Short answer: you. God has bound himself to you in his covenant of grace. God could have simply redeemed us for an eternity apart from sin and the curse. But instead, he brought us into fellowship with himself. He makes us his friends, objects of his special love. As Paul says in Ephesians, we are "his glorious inheritance" (1:18), the precious possession of Jesus himself.

If anything should sustain us in suffering, it is God's covenant of grace. In the midst of sorrow and suffering, the covenant of grace reminds us that God has redeemed us to draw us near and say, "I want you as my inheritance."

The Doctrine of the Sovereignty of God

God's sovereignty helps us bear up under the perplexities of life. Oh, that the Holy Spirit would work confidence in God's sovereignty deep into our bones. When we embrace God's sovereignty, we can stare down the worst suffering, the obscenities of sin, and the greatest wickedness in this fallen world and still confess with the hymn writer, "Whate'er my God ordains is right."[4]

The psalmist celebrates God's sovereignty in Psalm 89:8–13:

O LORD God of hosts,
> who is mighty as you are, O LORD,
> with your faithfulness all around you?
You rule the raging of the sea;
> when its waves rise, you still them.
You crushed Rahab like a carcass;
> you scattered your enemies with your mighty arm.
The heavens are yours; the earth also is yours;
> the world and all that is in it, you have founded them.
The north and the south, you have created them;
> Tabor and Hermon joyously praise your name.

You have a mighty arm;
>   strong is your hand, high your right hand.

God's sovereignty is indeed astounding. He raises and calms the sea. He covers the nations with morning and evening. He crushes the most powerful armies and lays hold of the powers of the created order. Our God can do anything—and he loves you. Because God is good, his sovereignty is a benevolent omnipotence, not a tyrannical one. God wields his sovereign power for the good of his people and for their ultimate blessing (Rom. 8:28).

We can dig in our nails and hang on even in the worst sorrow and pain because we know that God, the God who chose us and entered into covenant with us, is sovereign over all.

One Final Hope: The Gospel of Jesus Christ

Ultimately, we'll never appreciate this psalm fully until we see how it points to our Savior.

But now you have cast off and rejected;
>   you are full of wrath against your anointed.
You have renounced the covenant with your servant;
>   you have defiled his crown in the dust.
You have breached all his walls;
>   you have laid his strongholds in ruins.
All who pass by plunder him;
>   he has become the scorn of his neighbors.

You have exalted the right hand of his foes;
    you have made all his enemies rejoice.
You have also turned back the edge of his sword,
    and you have not made him stand in battle.
You have made his splendor to cease
    and cast his throne to the ground.
You have cut short the days of his youth;
    you have covered him with shame. (Ps. 89:38–45)

Psalm 89:38–45 is a picture of the dashed hopes of the people of God. They were promised that David and his line would reign forever, but now that promise seems to have failed.

Yet Scripture often shows us that what seems like a failure of God's promises is actually the very way he delivers on them. This description of David and his line cannot be exhausted by the experiences of David and his sons. Instead, these words are true, in the fullest sense, of David's greater son, the Lord Jesus Christ. How do we know?

The New Testament, on nearly every page, teaches that Jesus is the true and better David, the fulfillment of the Davidic covenant and the restorer of David's throne. Consider, for instance, Peter's sermon at Pentecost:

Men of Israel, hear these words: Jesus of Nazareth, a man attested to you by God with mighty works and wonders and signs that God did through him in your midst, as you yourselves know—this Jesus, delivered up according to the definite plan and foreknowledge of God, you crucified and killed by the hands of lawless men. God raised him up, loosing the pangs of death, because it was not possible for him to be held by it. For David says concerning him,

> "I saw the Lord always before me,
>> for he is at my right hand that I may not be
>>> shaken;
> therefore my heart was glad, and my tongue
>> rejoiced;
>> my flesh also will dwell in hope.
> For you will not abandon my soul to Hades,
>> or let your Holy One see corruption.
> You have made known to me the paths of life;
>> you will make me full of gladness with your
>>> presence."

Brothers, I may say to you with confidence about the patriarch David that he both died and was buried, and his tomb is with us to this day. Being therefore a prophet, and knowing that God had sworn with an oath to him that he would set one of his descendants on his throne, he foresaw and spoke about the resurrection of the Christ, that he was not abandoned to Hades, nor did his flesh see corruption. This Jesus God raised up, and of that we all are witnesses. (Acts 2:22–32)

As Peter explains, the psalms chronicling the suffering of David and his children are fully realized in the sufferings of Christ. David's flesh did, in fact, see corruption—he is, after all, still dead in his tomb. So, Peter reasons, this psalm must refer to David's greater son! Where did he get this idea? From the Lord Jesus himself. When Christ encountered the disciples on the road to Emmaus after his resurrection, he bemoaned that they did not see in the Old Testament the many evidences that Christ would undergo death and exile to restore what Adam and Israel had lost:

> And he said to them, "O foolish ones, and slow of heart to believe all that the prophets have spoken! Was it not necessary that the Christ should suffer these things and enter into his glory?" And beginning with Moses and all the Prophets, he interpreted to them in all the Scriptures the things concerning himself. (Luke 24:25–27)

The suffering of David and the people of Israel—rejection, curse, and judgment—were ultimately and consummately experienced by David's greater son, the servant of Israel, the Lord Jesus Christ.

Jesus experienced Psalm 89:38–45. And by that suffering Jesus restored the throne of David and saved the people of God. In God's mysterious providence, he delivered on his promises at the time when they seemed in greatest peril. Scripture attests repeatedly that God shows himself strong when circumstances seem most dire. In redemption, death always precedes resurrection. The cross always comes before the crown. Whatever catastrophe may end this world is merely a tool in God's hand to build the new heavens and the new earth. Whatever you fear may cause God's promises to fail will likely be the very thing he uses to fulfill them.

Peter's sermon in Acts 2 not only shows us that God fulfilled his promises through the suffering of Jesus; it reminds us that we are responsible for his death. Our sin nailed Jesus to the cross. And yet, Peter tells us to trust in him, this Jesus whom we killed, because it turns out that he died not for his sins but for ours. Hallelujah, what a Savior!

Psalm 89 gives us hope ultimately because it points us to the one who endured a suffering far beyond anything we will ever know. He was mocked and shamed and forsaken of God, so that we might be God's precious inheritance into eternity. Whatever suffering we may encounter, this gospel can carry us through it.

Notes

Foreword

1. Andrew Murray, quoted in Amy Carmichael, *Though the Mountains Shake* (Madras, India: Dohnavur Fellowship, 1943), 12.
2. Dr. and Mrs. Howard Taylor, *Hudson Taylor in Early Years: The Growth of a Soul* (Philadelphia: China Inland Mission, 1912), 291.

Chapter 1

1. John H. Walton, Victor H. Matthews, and Mark W. Chavalas, *The IVP Bible Background Commentary: Old Testament* (Downers Grove, IL: InterVarsity Press, 2000), 544.
2. Matthew Henry, *Matthew Henry's Commentary on the Whole Bible*, Christian Classics Ethereal Library, introductory comments on Ps. 88, http://www.ccel.org/ccel/henry/mhc3.Ps.lxxxix.html.
3. Carl Trueman, "What Can Miserable Christians Sing?," 9Marks, updated March 25, 2019, https://www.9marks.org/article/what-can-miserable -christians-sing/. This essay first appeared in Carl Trueman, *The Wages of Spin: Critical Writings on Historical and Contemporary Evangelicalism* (Fearn, Ross-Shire, Scotland: Christian Focus, 2004), 157–63.
4. Derek Kidner, *Psalms 73–150: A Commentary on Books III–V of the Psalms* (Downers Grove, IL: InterVarsity Press, 1973), 319.
5. Charles Simeon, *Horae Homileticae* (London: Holdsworth and Ball, 1832), 104.
6. K. [likely Robert Keen], "How Firm a Foundation," 1787.

Chapter 2

1. John Calvin, *Commentary on the Psalms*, vol. 1, Christian Classics Ethereal Library, preface, https://www.ccel.org/ccel/calvin/calcom08.vi.html.

2. James H. Fillmore (1849–1936), "I Will Sing of the Mercies of the Lord," ca. 1860s–1870s.

3. William Cowper (1731–1800), "God Moves in a Mysterious Way," 1774.

4. Samuel Rodigast (1649–1708), "Whate'er My God Ordains Is Right," 1675, trans. Catherine Winkworth (1827–1878), 1863.

General Index

Scripture Index

Scripture Index